FRANCIS LEDWIDGE
Selected Poems

Introduced by
SEAMUS HEANEY

Edited by
DERMOT BOLGER

**NEW
ISLAND**

Francis Ledwidge: Selected Poems
First published in 1992 and reprinted in June 2001 by
New Island
2 Brookside
Dundrum Road
Dublin 14
Ireland

ISBN 1 874597 10 3

The Arts Council
An Chomhairle Ealaíon

New Island receives financial support from The Arts Council
(An Chomhairle Ealaíon), Dublin, Ireland.

A catalogue record for this book is available from
The British Library.

Cover design by www.jonberkeley.com
Printed in Ireland by Colour Books Ltd.

CONTENTS

EDITOR'S NOTE

by Dermot Bolger

This volume fulfils a life long ambition to finally see in print a *Selected Poems* by Francis Ledwidge. In his own lifetime Ledwidge only saw one small volume of his poetry in print and was awaiting the appearance of his second, *Songs of Peace*, when he was killed by a stray shell on the 31 July 1917, while – in a cruel irony – working at the same job he had spent so much of his early manhood in Meath doing, building a road through mud near Ypres. *Songs of Peace*, which appeared three months later, was followed by *Last Songs*, edited – like the first two – by Lord Dunsany, and all three collections were quickly put together to form a *Complete Poems* which went through a number of editions between then and 1955.

This *Complete Poems* did however leave out a great deal of material which was either not to hand when Lord Dunsany was compiling his *Last Songs* or was not deemed strong enough by him. Alice Curtayne – to whom, like Seamus Heaney and anyone else interested in Francis Ledwidge, I owe a truly enormous debt for both her biography and for her work in collecting his missing poems – compiled a much extended *Complete Poems* in 1974, which served to reveal the full achievement of Francis Ledwidge as a poet. In a way though, it may have somewhat blurred that achievement also by highlighting the repetitiveness of so much of his work through presenting almost everything that he had ever written, and also by forsaking any chronological approach to the poems and instead grouping them under thematic headings like *Birds and Blossoms*, *Flights of Fancy* and *Months and Seasons*.

Ledwidge's first recorded poem was written at sixteen after he was sent by his mother to work as a grocer's apprentice to one Mr W.T. Daly in Rathfarnham. Consumed with homesickness one night he composed "Behind the Closed Eye" and was so moved by the experience that he abandoned his job to walk the thirty miles home to Slane through the dark, pausing to rest at each milestone along the way. Anyone writing at sixteen is generally yearning for any link of affinity to make one feel less alone. For me at that age Ledwidge's story had a special resonance because, overlooked by planners and on the edge of the Slane Road close to where I lived in Finglas, one such milestone still existed. At night I often sat there, feeling as uncertain of the future as most people that age are, and taking a curious solace from the fact that Ledwidge, at the same age and perhaps even more uncertain of his future, had rested upon the same stone under a similar dark sky.

Everything that Ledwidge had written I consumed with the uncritical openness of youth. I dreamt of, and finally made a pilgrimage to Slane (which now has his cottage turned into a museum and seats bearing the slogan "Ledwidge Country") and found the then deserted cottage where Ledwidge had lived (and was sheltered for the night by the artist Liam O'Brien whose studio is next door).

Returning sometimes to the writers of your youth can be dangerous and yet I find I am still greatly moved by the lyric grace and beauty of the best of Ledwidge's poetry. Much of his work suffers from the flaws of its time, the quality of advice given by a patron who was at once both deeply and generously concerned for him and yet blinkered enough to describe him as "a peasant" in the introduction to his first book, and the particular circumstances in which he came to public attention. One is frequently struck by the dichotomy between the physical details of his own life and the themes of his work. One can only guess at what sort of writer might have returned from that war and lived through the war that was to quickly follow in his own country. One can only guess also at what sort of century he would have foresaw ahead of him and whether he would have imagined the further irony that, seventy five years after his death, the landscape of Serbia – where he both fought and wrote poetry of clarity and beauty – would again be synonymous in the public mind with war.

In making this selection of the best of his work I have regrouped the poems back into their original three volumes and added in a number of fine poems uncovered by Alice Curtayne (marked by the initials C.P. for *Complete Poems*) where I feel they roughly belong in time. In *Songs of Peace* either Ledwidge or Dunsany had grouped the poems according to where they were written and I have added these locations (along with some others and some dates) in brackets. The dates of the three books refer to when they appeared only and are not a guide to when the poems were written. *Songs of the Fields* was compiled and the introduction written in the peaceful summer of 1914 in Meath, but did not appear until the winter of 1915 when Ledwidge was dug into a bitterly cold mountain ridge in Serbia on starvation rations of one tin of bully beef between four men per day and two army biscuits each.

One poem out of sequence is "A Little Boy in the Morning", a superb elegy for a young Slane boy, Jack Tiernan, who – like Ledwidge at his age – used to drive cattle for local farmers. If "Thomas McDonagh" is so often retrospectively read as a lament for the adult Ledwidge himself, then I feel this poem – written while home of leave – is as suitable an epitaph for the young Ledwidge, rushing with his brother after school to join their mother stooping at work in the frosty dusk of other men's fields, walking home together through the dark listening to her songs and stories, already with the gift of poetry forming in his head. Did that child ever dream that long after the rich men of his youth were forgotten, over a century later the youth of Slane would gather in the evenings on benches which commemorate him; that long after many of the great writers of his time were equally forgotten, so many ordinary people would pause on that bridge over the Boyne to recall the lines of poetry he would later compose and which, for so long in his life, were the only things he truly owned?

Dermot Bolger,
October 1992.

INTRODUCTION

by Seamus Heaney

It was appropriate that the excellent biography of Francis Ledwidge which appeared in 1972 should have been written by Alice Curtayne, a scholar noted more for her works on religious subjects than for her literary studies. Even though Ms Curtayne did once publish a study of Dante, her name, like Ledwidge's, evokes a certain nostalgia for those decades when this poet was appropriated and gratefully cherished as the guarantor of an Ireland domesticated, pious and demure; his poems used to be a safe bet for the convent library and the school prize, a charm against all that modernity which threatened the traditional values of a country battening down for independence. But Ledwidge's fate had been more complex and more modern than that. He very deliberately chose not to bury his head in local sand and, as a consequence, faced the choices and moral challenges of his times with solitude, honesty and rare courage. This integrity, and its ultimately gratifying effects upon his poetry, should command the renewed interest and respect of Irish people at the present time: Ledwidge lived through a similar period of historical transition when political, cultural and constitutional crises put into question values which had previously appeared as ratified and immutable as the contours of the land itself.

A lot of Irish people can still quote at least one line of his poetry. "He shall not hear the bittern cry," they say, and then memory falters until the final image of "Thomas McDonagh" comes back, and they make a stab at something about the Dark Cow "lifting her horn in pleasant meads". For many of these people, Ledwidge vaguely belongs to the moment of 1916 and his note plays in with poems like Joseph Mary Plunkett's "I see his blood upon the rose" and Padraig Pearse's "Mise Eire", so that he is conceived of as somebody who "sang to sweeten Ireland's wrong". But for others, the abiding impression left by this poet is one of political ambivalence. For these people, the salient factor is his enlistment in the British Army in 1914 and his being in its tanks during the Easter Rising, in the uniform of those who executed, among others, Thomas McDonagh. The blame for this inconvenient *shoneenism*, however, is then laid at the aristocratic feet of Lord Dunsany, Ledwidge's most helpful mentor, literary agent and patron, so that in this scenario the poet shows up as a naïve patriot betrayed by the scheming Unionist peer into an act that went against his truest dispositions and convictions.

As Alice Curtayne's biography (to which I am here greatly indebted) makes clear, neither of these versions will do. To see him as the uncomplicated voice of romantic nationalism misrepresents the agonized consciousness which held in balance and ultimately decided between the command to act upon the dictates of a morality he took to be both objective and universally applicable, and the desire to keep faith with a politically resistant and particularly contentious Irish line. To see him as the dupe of a socially superior and politically insidious West British toff is to underrate his intelligence, his independence and the consciously fatal nature of his decision to enlist. For Ledwidge was no wilting flower; as James Stephens wrote of him:

I met him twice and then only for a few minutes. He is what we call here 'a lump of a lad 'and he was panoplied in all the protective devices, or disguises, which a countryman puts on when he meets a man of the town!

This is the Ledwidge who is now commemorated by a plaque placed first on the bridge over the River Boyne at Slane, and then on the restored labourer's cottage ouside the village where he was born on 19 August 1887, the second youngest in a surviving family of four brothers and three sisters. That the plaque appeared on the bridge first rather than the house has a certain appropriateness also, since the bridge, like the poet, was actually and symbolically placed between two Irelands.

Upstream, then and now, were situated several pleasant and potent reminders of an anglicized, assimilated country: the Marquis of Conyngham's parkland sweeping down to the artfully wooded banks of the river, the waters of the river itself pouring their delicious sheen over the weir; Slane Castle and the big house at Beauparc; the canal and the towpath – here was an Irish landscape in which a young man like Ledwidge would be as likely to play cricket (he did) as Gaelic football (which he did also). The whole scene was as composed and historical as a topographical print, and possessed the tranquil allure of the established order of nineteenth century, post-union Ireland. Downstream, however, there were historical and prehistorical reminders of a different sort which operated as a strong counter-establishment influence in the young Ledwidge's mind. The Boyne battlefield, the megalithic tombs at Newgrange, Knowth and Dowth, the Celtic burying ground at Rosnaree – these things were beginning to be construed as part of the mystical body of an Irish culture which had suffered mutilation and was in need of restoration. Ledwidge would also have known about local associations with St Patrick, Cormac Mac Airt, Aengus the love god and many other legendary figures; and not far away was the Hill of Tara, where his mother filled his mind with the usual lore:

That old mill, built on the site of the first cornmill ever erected in Ireland, used to belong to my father's people when everybody had their own and these broad acres and leopard-coloured woods, almost as far as Kilcairne, all these were ours one time.

In a fairly obvious way then, the map of the field of Ledwidge's affections reflected the larger map of the conflicting cultural and political energies which were operative in Ireland throughout his lifetime. Furthermore, it could be argued that the weaker, nambier side of his poetry represents both a simplification of this divided predicament and a compensation for it. There is something regressive in the way he often seems to be holding on to the skirts of a maternal landscape. His melodiousness can at times verge upon the infantile and, indeed, a conventional Oedipal reading of Ledwidge's temperament makes a lot of sense. Not only did he project the mother into the scenes around him, but he was also conspicuously hampered in his relationships with the two young women he fell for. He was content enough romping round *ceilidhes* and football matches ana *feiseanna* with other young men, indulging in the horseplay that never mutates into foreplay; he was popular, handsome and noticeable; long before it was fashionable, he wore a tweed suit, and once his first book of poems had been accepted for publication he affected a flowing Byronic necktie. But for all his dash, he was unforceful and sentimental when it came to his two romances, first with Ellie Vaughey, the daughter of a local farmer, and then Lizzie Healy, a sister of the schoolteacher in Slane. Deeply attached as he was to Ellie, he seems to have accepted their separation as inevitable when her parents insisted she stop seeing him because he was socially a cut beneath her. (She would marry a farmer called O'Neill) And with Lizzie, a lot of time seems to have been spent in tiffs about a bunch of violets which he had sent her on Valentine's day and a poem which he had not published in the *Meath Chronicle*. It is significant, indeed, that it was only after Ellie died that Ledwidge seems to have been emotionally and artistically capable of dealing with the experience by imagining her (typically) into flowers of the field.

Ledwidge did achieve a detached and tested selfhood, but not by the Joycean method of rejection. The pathos of a poem like "My Mother", is a far cry from the imaginative detachment evident in the presentation of Mrs Dedalus in *Ulysses*; and yet the poem is not without its own touches of self-awareness. The lines about her "earthly lover" who "kissed away the music from her lips" nicely evoke the figure of the wife martyred to domestic life, enduring the death of personality in the birth of familial responsibility (Ledwidge's father died when he was four and the mother did constant housework and field work right up until the poet's early manhood). Furthermore, the poet's recognition of his own emotional timidities and capitulations are very wistfully rendered in the accurate if indulgent self-portrait with which the poem ends: "This poor bird-hearted singer of a day".

Ledwidge would not attain victory over the birdheartedness until the conflicting energies of his times and his temperament found themselves in alignment. Much in him that was ready to break out remained beyond the reach of his writing. He could bring the instinctive nostalgic Celtic side of Slane life to literary fruition in a poem like "The wife of Llew" but a gap remained between the genteel idiom which he understandably foisted on himself and the local life which he totally and unself-consciously embodied. He might read Longfellow, have literary exchanges with the curate like one Father Smyth, discourse and share poems in manuscript with his fiddler friend, Matty McGoona, send work out to the *Drogheda Independent*, but this side of his doings must have seemed disjunct from much else that was significant and central to his own and his generation's experience. The Keatsian idiom he inherited and Dunsany's ambitions for him as a writer had not much to do with his work as a road surfacerman, his work in the coppermines of Beauparc, his involvement with trade-union politics there and eventual dismissal for organizing a strike against bad conditions; his fights at football matches in Navan; his participation in amateur dramatics; his activity as a member of Navan Rural Council, as a worker in an insurance office in that town and as secretary of the Irish Volunteers when they were eventually set up in Slane.

The character who was fit for all this was obviously much more robust than the writing in many of his poems would suggest. Not only did the salon idiom put him at some debilitated distance from himself, but the one tradition he naturally possessed – that of the local ballad of love and or exile – was artistically too naïve to encompass the things that would happen to him. When Ledwidge was on board ship for Gallipoli, for example, he wrote "Crockaharna", which represents this poet at his worst – even if it is a worst which is in an odd way authentic, all of a piece with recitations and party-pieces at *Ceilidhe* houses like the McGoona's, continuous with the tenor on the stage at the variety concert.

Lord Dunsany, in fact, was not capable of bringing Ledwidge all that far beyond this. Obviously, he was practically extremely generous and well disposed, arranging for the publication of his books and writing introductions to them; but as a critic, he was capable of little beyond scolding his protegé for pretentious or archaic poeticisms. What he did do, however, was to introduce Ledwidge to his own Irish contemporaries in the craft, people such as Thomas McDonagh, Padraic Colum, James Stephens, AE, Oliver St John Gogarty. These writers had ideas about the specific challenges and developments which were opening up for poetry in Ireland, and had produced work that gave credence to the idea that the creation of a distinctive Irish literature in English was under way. By putting Ledwidge in touch with them, Dunsany did open the doors of perception and self awareness wider than the young poet might have managed on his own. Poems on mythological themes, very Yeatsian performances, admittedly began to appear and a finer, more objective way with verse-craft began to be in evidence (as in, for example, "The Wife of Llew").

Yet for a long time, Ledwidge did not really have a compelling theme. According to W.B.Yeats's famous phrase, it is out of "the quarrel with ourselves" that poetry comes, and it was only when this particular inner quarrel flared and could not be placated or resolved that Ledwidge's full force, as a personality, a poet and a morally sensitive creature, became engaged. This happened after John Redmond's epoch-making speech at Woodenbridge on 20 September 1913, a speech which split the Irish Volunteers and put a cruel strain on Ledwidge. He was, after all, an office bearer of the organization at local level and imaginatively susceptible to the honourable motives behind both Redmond's breakaway National Volunteers (willing to be recruited to the British War effort) and the recalcitrant rump of the Irish Volunteers (who stuck to a more separatist reading of the Volunteers' original pledge "to secure and maintain the rights and loyalties common to the whole people of Ireland"). The formation of the Irish Volunteers in the first place had been a direct response to the formation of the Ulster Volunteers, so even though the ideal they were meant to defend was Home Rule by Parliamentary process, they were still part of the surge towards Irish independence

16

that had grown more definite in the years before 1914. Thus, when Redmond urged them "to drill and make themselves efficient for the work ... not only in Ireland itself, but wherever the firing line extends in defence of rights of freedom and religion in this war," he was radically complicating the issue for everybody involved.

Ledwidge held out with the rump. At Navan Rural Council, on 10 October 1914, he would not be associated with a motion congratulating Redmond. Nine days later, he was the only member to hold out against the general agreement within the Rural Council to rescind its advertising contracts with *The Volunteer*, the organ of the pre-split movement, now continuing in rivalry to Redmond's paper, *The National Volunteer*. The prevailing mood of the movement was expressed in council by several of the members:

Mr Bowens: The young men of Meath would be better off fighting on the fields of France for the future of Ireland. That was his opinion, and he would remark that he was sorry to see there in the town of Navan – and probably in the village of Slane where Mr Ledwidge came from – ... a few Sinn Feiners that followed the tail end of MacNeill's party. There was nothing but strife in the country as long as these people had anything to do with the country ... What was England's uprise would be also Ireland's uprise.

(Applause)

Mr Ledwidge: England's uprise has always been Ireland's downfall.

Mr Owens: ... What was he (Mr Ledwidge)? Was he an Irishman or a pro-German?

Mr Ledwidge: I am an anti-German and an Irishman.

Five days after these exchanges, Francis Ledwidge enlisted in the Royal Inniskilling Fusiliers at Richmond Barracks. Some say because Ellie Vaughey was going to marry John O' Neill, which could have been part of the reason. Some say because Lord Dunsany coaxed him, which he almost certainly did not. I am tempted to say what Ledwidge himself said after the event:

I joined the British Army because she stood between Ireland and an enemy common to our civilization and I would not have her say that she defended us while we did nothing at home but pass resolutions.

17

This is surely one of the rare occasions in English when an army is given the feminine gender, and it prompts one to speculate that Ledwidge's solidarity in the ranks was a further acting out of his identification with the hard years which his mother had done in the field on his behalf, an instance of compulsion to acknowledge such service with a corresponding gesture of self-sacrifice. At any rate, the statement makes it clear that Ledwidge acted with premeditation and out of a conflict of feelings. A sense of honour, a rage of exasperation, a preconscious compulsion: whatever the reason, it propelled him through the hell of campaigns on three fronts, first at Gallipoli, then in the Balkans and finally in the trenches and dug-outs of Ypres where he was killed by an exploding shell on 31 July, 1917.

Meanwhile, at Easter 1916, England's difficulty had been Ireland's opportunity. The rising occurred, the leaders were shot and the mood of the country began to change. As it did, Ledwidge's mood darkened also. On 20 April that year, on his way back to Ireland for a sick leave after a devastating retreat march to Salonika, Ledwidge could write to Dunsany:

Coming from Southhampton in the train, looking on England's beautiful valleys all white with spring, I thought indeed its freedom was worth all the blood I have seen flow. No wonder England has so many ardent patriots. I would be one of them myself did I not presume to be an Irish patriot.

A couple of weeks later, while he was convalescing in Slane, Ledwidge's equanimity would be shattered. In Richmond Barracks, where he enlisted, Thomas McDonagh and Joseph Mary Plunkett would be sentenced to death and then executed at Arbour Hill by soldiers in the uniform he had elected to wear as an act of Irish patriotism.

It is needless to elaborate on the pain of all this and not surprising to find him being court-martialled during this same leave for offensive remarks to a superior officer. He drank more than usual. He reported late for duty. But he did not desert. Instead, he wrote the poem by which he is best remembered, "Thomas McDonagh", and harnessed his patriotic impulse to the task of sounding the Irish note which McDonagh himself

had discovered in Irish poetry and had to some extent prescribed
for it. His new command of the Gaelic techniques of assonance
and internal rhyme constituted an oblique declaration of loyalty
to a complex of feelings not represented by the uniform in
which he fought. Ledwidge would go on to write other poems in
the aftermath of 1916, all of them showing more point and bite
than his early nature lyrics but none of them as perfect a
realization of his gifts as this one. It is a poem in which his
displaced hankering for the place beyond confusion and his own
peculiar melancholy voice find a subject which exercises them
entirely, no doubt because in lamenting McDonagh he was to a
large extent lamenting himself:

He shall not hear the bittern cry
In the wild sky, where he is lain,
Nor voices of the sweeter birds
Above the wailing of the rain.

Nor shall he know when loud March blows
Thro' slanting snows her fanfare shrill,
Blowing to flame the golden cup
Of many an upset daffodil.

But when the Dark Cow leaves the moor,
And pastures poor with greedy weeds,
Perhaps he'll hear her low at morn
Lifting her horn in pleasant meads.

Ledwidge solved nothing. As a poet, his sense of purpose and
his own gifts were only beginning to come into mature focus. As
a political phenomenon, he represents conflicting elements in
the Irish inheritance which continue to be repressed or
unresolved. There is still minimal public acknowledgement in
Ireland of the part played by Irish soldiers in the First World
War, although their devotion to the ideal of independence was
passionate in its day; and we do now see the development of a
corresponding unwillingness to acknowledge the heroic aspect

of the 1916 Rising. Perhaps, too, the meaning of his choice has lost resonance because the concept of personal integrity as a relevant factor in political decision has been gradually eroding: a Marxist-influenced consensus tends to put the onus on the individual to make a correct theoretical assessment of what is historically progressive rather than act upon some internalized moral principle. Nevertheless, the combination of vulnerability and adequacy which Ledwidge displayed in facing the life of his times remains admirable and as people in Ireland today prepare to encounter the dilemmas of their own times – moral, constitutional, domestic, international – his example constitutes a challenge to act with solitary resolve and to expect neither consensus nor certitude.

In the literary reckoning, Yeat's Irish airman foreseeing his death with an absolved exhilaration – "A lovely impulse of delight/Led to this tumult in the clouds" – may manifest both the triumph and the immunity of greater artistic genius: in such company, Ledwidge is neither a very strong nor a very original talent. Yet this "bird-hearted singer" keeps the nest warm and the lines open for a different poetry, one that might combine tendermindedness towards the predicaments of others with an ethically unsparing attitude towards the self. Indeed, it is because of this scruple, this incapacity for grand and overbearing certainties, and not because of the uniform he wore, it is for this reason that Ledwidge can be counted as a "war poet" in the company of Wilfred Owen and Siegfried Sassoon. Yet his status as a combatant is finally not as important as his membership of the company of the walking wounded, wherever they are to be found at any given time.

A LITTLE BOY IN THE MORNING

He will not come, and still I wait.
He whistles at another gate
Where angels listen. Ah, I know
He will not come, yet if I go
How shall I know he did not pass
Barefooted in the flowery grass?

The moon leans on one silver horn
Above the silhouettes of morn,
And from their nest-sills finches whistle
Or stooping pluck the downy thistle.
How is the morn so gay and fair
Without his whistling in its air?

The world is calling, I must go.
How shall I know he did not pass
Barefooted in the shining grass?

S. O. P.
(*At Home*)

Songs of the Fields
(1915)

BEHIND THE CLOSED EYE

I walk the old frequented ways
  That wind around the tangled braes,
I live again the sunny days
  Ere I the city knew.

And scenes of old again are born,
  The woodbine lassoing the thorn,
And drooping Ruth-like in the corn
  The poppies weep the dew.

Above me in their hundred schools
  The magpies bend their young to rules,
And like an apron full of jewels
  The dewy cobweb swings.

And frisking in the stream below
  The troutlets make the circles flow,
And the hungry crane doth watch them grow
  As a smoker does his rings.

Above me smokes the little town,
  With its whitewashed walls and roofs of brown
And its octagon spire toned smoothly down
  As the holy minds within.

And wondrous impudently sweet,
  Half of him passion, half conceit,
The blackbird calls adown the street
  Like the piper of Hamelin.

I hear him, and I feel the lure
   Drawing me back to the homely moor,
I'll go and close the mountains' door
   On the city's strife and din.

(1902)

A TWILIGHT IN MIDDLE MARCH

Within the oak a throb of pigeon wings
Fell silent, and grey twilight hushed the fold,
And spiders' hammocks swung on half-oped things
That shook like foreigners upon our cold.
A gipsy lit a fire and made a sound
Of moving tins, and from an oblong moon
The river seemed to gush across the ground
To the cracked metre of a marching tune.

And then three syllables of melody
Dropped from a blackbird's flute, and died apart
Far in the dewy dark. No more but three,
Yet sweeter music never touched a heart
'Neath the blue domes of London. Flute and reed,
Suggesting feelings of the solitude
When will was all the Delphi I would heed,
Lost like a wind within a summer wood
From little knowledge where great sorrows brood.

(1914)

DESIRE IN SPRING

I love the cradle songs that mothers sing
In lonely places when the twilight drops,
The slow endearing melodies that bring
Sleep to the weeping lids; and, when she stops,
I love the roadside birds upon the tops
Of dusty hedges in a world of Spring.

And when the sunny rain drips from the edge
Of midday wind, and meadows lean one way,
And a long whisper passes thro' the sedge,
Beside the broken water let me stay,
While these old airs upon my memory play,
And silent changes colour up the hedge.

(1914)

28

MAY MORNING

Young May came peeping o'er the mount
And dressed herself before the font.
The glow-worm snuffed his candle bright.
The brooklet tumbled into light.
The skylark sang into the blue.
The baby corn sprang into view.
The merle piped beside the rill.
The mavis answered from the hill
The daisy crowned each grassy bleb.
The spider crossed his dewy web.
The wood-pecker the hazel tapped
And straight its little leaves unwrapped.
The snipe forsook his marshy bed.
The ceannabawn raised up its head
And still the harper played away
The march of morning into day.

C.P.
(*Drogheda Independent, 1912*)

JUNE

Broom out the floor now, lay the fender by,
And plant this bee-sucked bough of woodbine there,
And let the window down. The butterfly
Floats in upon the sunbeam, and the fair
Tanned face of June, the nomad gipsy, laughs
Above her widespread wares, the while she tells
The farmers' fortunes in the fields, and quaffs
The water from the spider-peopled wells.

The hedges are all drowned in green grass seas,
And bobbing poppies flare like Elmo's light,
While siren-like the pollen-stained bees
Drone in the clover depths. And up the height
The cuckoo's voice is hoarse and broke with joy.
And on the lowland crops the crows make raid,
Nor fear the clappers of the farmer's boy,
Who sleeps, like drunken Noah, in the shade.

And loop this red rose in that hazel ring
That snares your little ear, for June is short
And we must joy in it and dance and sing,
And from her bounty draw her rosy worth.
Ay! soon the swallows will be flying south,
The wind wheel north to gather in the snow,
Even the roses spilt on youth's red mouth
Will soon blow down the road all roses go.

AUGUST

She'll come at dusky first of day,
White over yellow harvest's song.
Upon her dewy rainbow way
She shall be beautiful and strong.
The lidless eye of noon shall spray
Tan on her ankles in the hay,
Shall kiss her brown the whole day long.

I'll know her in the windows, tall
Above the crickets of the hay.
I'll know her when her odd eyes fall,
One May-blue, one November-grey.
I'll watch her down the red barn wall
Take down her rusty scythe, and call,
And I will follow her away.

THE HILLS

The hills are crying from the fields to me,
And calling me with music from a choir
Of waters in their woods where I can see
The bloom unfolded on the whins like fire.
And, as the evening moon climbs ever higher
And blots away the shadows from the slope,
They cry to me like things devoid of hope.

Pigeons are home. Day droops. The fields are cold.
Now a slow wind comes labouring up the sky.
With a small cloud long steeped in sunset gold,
Like Jason with the precious fleece anigh
The harbour of Iolcos. Day's bright eye
Is filmed with the twilight, and the rill
Shines like a scimitar upon the hill.

And moonbeams drooping thro' the coloured wood
Are full of little people winged white.
I'll wander thro' the moon-pale solitude
That calls across the intervening night
With river voices at their utmost height,
Sweet as rain-water in the blackbird's flute
That strikes the world in admiration mute.

THE WIFE OF LLEW

And Gwydion said to Math, when it was Spring:
"Come now and let us make a wife for Llew."
And so they broke broad boughs yet moist with dew,
And in a shadow made a magic ring:
They took the violet and the meadowsweet
To form her pretty face, and for her feet
They built a mound of daisies on a wing,
And for her voice they made a linnet sing
In the wide poppy blowing for her mouth.
And over all they chanted twenty hours.
And Llew came singing from the azure south
And bore away his wife of birds and flowers.

TO A LINNET IN A CAGE

When Spring is in the fields that stained your wing,
  And the blue distance is alive with song,
And finny quiets of the gabbling spring
  Rock lilies red and long,
At dewy daybreak, I will set you free
  In ferny turnings of the woodbine lane,
Where faint-voiced echoes leave and cross in glee
  The hilly swollen plain.

In draughty houses you forget your tune,
  The modulator of the changing hours.
You want the wide air of the moody noon,
  And the slanting evening showers.
So I will loose you, and your song shall fall
  When morn is white upon the dewy pane,
Across my eyelids, and my soul recall
  From worlds of sleeping pain.

THOUGHTS AT THE TRYSTING STILE

Come, May, and hang a white flag on each thorn,
Make truce with earth and heaven; the April child
Now hides her sulky face deep in the morn
Of your new flowers by the water wild
And in the ripples of the rising grass,
And rushes bent to let the south wind pass
On with her tumult of swift nomad wings,
And broken domes of downy dandelion.
Only in spasms now the blackbird sings.
The hour is all a-dream.
     Nets of woodbine
Throw woven shadows over dreaming flowers,
And dreaming, a bee-luring lily bends
Its tender bell where blue dyke-water cowers
Thro' briars and folded ferns, and gripping ends
Of wild convolvulus.

      The lark's sky-way
Is desolate.
    I watch an apple-spray
Beckon across a wall as if it knew
I wait the calling of the orchard maid.
Inly I feel that she will come in blue,
With yellow on her hair, and two curls strayed
Out of her comb's loose stocks, and I shall steal
Behind and lay my hands upon her eyes,
"Look not, but be my Psyche!"
       And her peal
Of laughter will ring far, and as she tries
For freedom I will call her names of flowers

That climb up walls; then thro' the twilight hours
We'll talk about the loves of ancient queens,
And kisses like wasp-honey, false and sweet,
And how we are entangled in love's snares
Like wind-looped flowers.

BEFORE THE TEARS

You looked as sad as an eclipsed moon
Above the sheaves of harvest, and there lay
A light lisp on your tongue, and very soon
The petals of your deep blush fell away;
White smiles that come with an uneasy grace
From inner sorrow crossed your forehead fair,
When the wind passing took your scattered hair
And flung it like a brown shower in my face.

Tear-fringed winds that fill the heart's low sighs
And never break upon the bosom's pain,
But blow unto the windows of the eyes
Their misty promises of silver rain,
Around your loud heart ever rose and fell.
I thought 'twere better that the tears should come
And strike your every feeling wholly numb,
So thrust my hand in yours and shook farewell.

ALL-HALLOWS EVE

The dreadful hour is sighing for a moon
  To light old lovers to the place of tryst,
And old footsteps from blessed acres soon
  On old known pathways will be lightly prest;
And winds that went to eavesdrop since the noon,
  Kinking at some old tale told sweetly brief,
  Will give a cowslick to the yarrow leaf,
And sling the round nut from the hazel down.

And there will be old yarn-balls, and old spells
  In broken lime-kilns, and old eyes will peer
For constant lovers in old spidery wells,
  And old embraces will grow newly dear,
And some may meet old lovers in old dells.
  And some in doors ajar in towns light-lorn;
  But two will meet beneath a gnarly thorn
Deep in the bosom of the windy fells.

Then when the night slopes home and white-faced day
  Yawns in the east there will be sad farewells;
And many feet will tap a lonely way
  Back to the comfort of their chilly cells,
And eyes will backward turn and long to stay
  Where love first found them in the clover bloom –
  But one will never seek the lonely tomb,
And two will linger at the tryst alway.

A FEAR

I roamed the woods to-day and seemed to hear,
As Dante heard, the voice of suffering trees.
The twisted roots seemed bare contorted knees,
The bark was full of faces strange with fear.

I hurried home still wrapt in that dark spell,
And all the night upon the world's great lie
I pondered, and a voice seemed whisp'ring high,
"You died long since, and all this thing is hell!"

BEFORE THE WAR OF COOLEY

At daybreak Maeve rose up from where she prayed
And took her prophetess across her door
To gaze upon her hosts. Tall spear and blade
Burnished for early battle dimly shook
The morning's colours, and then Maeve said:
                                        "Look
And tell me how you see them now."
                                        And then
The woman that was lean with knowledge said:
"There's crimson on them, and there's dripping red."
And a tall soldier galloped up the glen
With foam upon his boot, and halted there
Beside old Maeve. She said, "Not yet," and turned
Into her blazing dun, and knelt in prayer
One solemn hour, and once again she came
And sought her prophetess. With voice that mourned
"How do you see them now?" she asked.
                                        "All lame
And broken in the noon." And once again
The soldier stood before her.

                                        "No, not yet."
Maeve answered his inquiring look and turned
Once more unto her prayer, and yet once more
"How do you see them now?" she asked.
                                        "All wet
With storm rains, and all broken, and all tore
With midnight wolves." And when the soldier came
Maeve said, "It is the hour." There was a flash
Of trumpets in the dim, a silver flame

Of rising shields, loud words passed down the ranks,
And twenty feet they saw the lances leap.
They passed the dun with one short noisy dash.
And turning proud Maeve gave the wise one thanks,
And sought her chamber in the dun to weep.

GOD'S REMEMBRANCE

There came a whisper from the night to me
Like music of the sea, a mighty breath
From out the valley's dewy mouth, and Death
Shook his lean bones, and every coloured tree
Wept in the fog of morning. From the town
Of nests among the branches one old crow
With gaps upon his wings flew far away.
And, thinking of the golden summer glow,
I heard a blackbird whistle half his lay
Among the spinning leaves that slanted down.

And I who am a thought of God's now long
Forgotten in His Mind, and desolate
With other dreams long over, as a gate
Singing upon the wind the anvil song,
Sang of the Spring when first He dreamt of me
In that old town all hills and signs that creak:
And He remembered me as something far
In old imaginations, something weak
With distance, like a little sparkling star
Drowned in the lavender of evening sea.

THE VISION ON THE BRINK

To-night when you sit in the deep hours alone,
   And from the sleeps you snatch wake quick and feel
You hear my step upon the threshold-stone,
   My hand upon the doorway latchward steal,
Be sure 'tis but the white winds of the snow,
   For I shall come no more.

And when the candle in the pane is wore,
   And moonbeams down the hill long shadows throw,
When night's white eyes are in the chinky door,
   Think of a long road in a valley low,
Think of a wanderer in the distance far,
   Lost like a voice among the scattered hills.

And when the moon has gone and oceans spills
   Its waters backward from the trysting bar,
And in dark furrows of the night there tills
   A jewelled plough, and many a falling star
Moves you to prayer, then will you think of me
   On the long road that will not ever end.

Jonah is hoarse in Nineveh – I'd lend
   My voice to save the town – and hurriedly
Goes Abraham with murdering knife, and Ruth
   Is weary in the corn…. Yet will I stay,
For one flower blooms upon the rocks of truth,
   God is in all our hurry and delay.

WAITING

A strange old woman on the wayside sate,
Looking far away and shook her head and sighed.
And when anon, close by, a rusty gate
Loud on the warm winds cried,
She lifted up her eyes and said, "You're late."
Then shook her head and sighed.

And evening found her thus, and night in state
Walked thro' the starlight, and a heavy tide
Followed the yellow moon around her wait,
And morning walked in wide.
She lifted up her eyes and said "You're late."
Then shook her head and sighed.

Songs of Peace
(1917)

THE PLACE

Blossoms as old as May I scatter here,
And a blue wave I lifted from the stream.
It shall not know when winter days are drear
Or March is hoarse with blowing. But a-dream
The laurel boughs shall hold a canopy
Peacefully over it the winter long,
Till all the birds are back from oversea,
And April rainbows win a blackbird's song.

And when the war is over I shall take
My lute a-down to it and sing again
Songs of the whispering things amongst the brake,
And those I love shall know them by their strain.
Their airs shall be the blackbird's twilight song,
Their words shall be all flowers with fresh dews hoar.
But it is lonely now in winter long,
And, God! to hear the blackbird sing once more.

(In Barracks)

47

MAY

She leans across an orchard gate somewhere,
Bending from out the shadows to the light,
A dappled spray of blossom in her hair
Studded with dew-drops lovely from the night
She smiles to think how many hearts she'll smite
With beauty ere her robes fade from the lawn,
She hears the robin's cymbals with delight,
The skylarks in the rosebush of the dawn.

For her the cowslip rings its yellow bell,
For her the violets watch with wide blue eyes.
The wandering cuckoo doth its clear name tell
Thro' the white mist of blossoms where she lies
Painting a sunset for the western skies.
You'd know her by her smile and by her tear
And by the way the swift and martin flies,
Where she is south of these wild days and drear.

(In Barracks)

48

TO EILISH OF THE FAIR HAIR

I'd make my heart a harp to play for you
Love songs within the evening dim of day,
Were it not dumb with ache and with mildew
Of sorrow withered like a flower away,
It hears so many calls from homeland places,
So many sighs from all it will remember,
From the pale roads and woodlands where your face is
Like laughing sunlight running thro' December.

But this it singeth loud above its pain,
To bring the greater ache: whate'er befall
The love that oft-times woke the sweeter strain
Shall turn to you always. And should you call
To pity it some day in those old places
Angels will covet the loud joy that fills it.
But thinking of the by-ways where your face is
Sunlight on other hearts—Ah! how it kills it.

(In Barracks)

THE GARDENER

Among the flowers, like flowers, her slow hands move
Easing a muffled bell or stooping low
To help sweet roses climb the stakes above,
Where pansies stare and seem to whisper "Lo!"
Like gaudy butterflies her sweet peas blow
Filling the garden with dim rustlings. Clear
On the sweet Book she reads how long ago
There was a garden to a woman dear.

She makes her life one grand beatitude
Of Love and Peace, and with contented eyes
She sees not in the whole world mean or rude,
And her small lot she trebly multiplies.
And when the darkness muffles up the skies
Still to be happy is her sole desire,
She sings sweet songs about a great emprise,
And sees a garden blowing in the fire.

(At Sea)

LULLABY

Shall I take the rainbow out of the sky
And the moon from the well in the lane,
And break them in pieces to coax your eye
To slumber a wee while again?
Rock goes the cradle, and rock, and rock.
The mouse has stopped nibbling under the clock
And the crows have gone home to Slane.

The little lambs came from the hills of brown,
With pillows of wool for your fair little head.
And the birds from the bushes flew in with down
To make you snug in your cradle bed.
Rock goes the cradle, and rock, and rock.
The mouse has stopped nibbling under the clock.
And the birds and the lambs have fled.

There is wind from the bog. It will blow all night,
Upsetting the willows and scattering rain.
The poor little lambs will be crying with fright
For the kind little birds in the hedge of the lane.
Rock goes the cradle, and rock, and rock.
Sleep, little one, sleep, and the wet wind mock,
Till the crows come back from Slane.

C.P.
(1915)

THE HOME-COMING OF THE SHEEP

The sheep are coming home in Greece,
Hark the bells on every hill!
Flock by flock, and fleece by fleece,
Wandering wide a little piece
Thro' the evening red and still,
Stopping where the pathways cease,
Cropping with a hurried will.

Thro' the cotton-bushes low
Merry boys with shouldered crooks
Close them in a single row,
Shout among them as they go
With one bell-ring o'er the brooks.
Such delight you never know
Reading it from gilded books.

Before the early stars are bright
Cormorants and sea-gulls call,
And the moon comes large and white
Filling with a lovely light
The ferny curtained waterfall.
Then sleep wraps every bell up tight
And the climbing moon grows small.

(In Greece)

MY MOTHER

God made my mother on an April day,
From sorrow and the mist along the sea,
Lost birds' and wanderers' songs and ocean spray,
And the moon loved her wandering jealously.

Beside the ocean's din she combed her hair,
Singing the nocturne of the passing ships,
Before her earthly lover found her there
And kissed away the music from her lips.

She came unto the hills and saw the change
That brings the swallow and the geese in turns.
But there was not a grief she deemed strange,
For there is that in her which always mourns.

Kind heart she has for all on hill or wave
Whose hopes grew wings like ants to fly away.
I bless the God Who such a mother gave
This poor bird-hearted singer of a day.

(In Hospital In Egypt)

TO ONE DEAD

A blackbird singing
On a moss-upholstered stone,
Bluebells swinging,
Shadows wildly blown,
A song in the wood,
A ship on the sea.
The song was for you
and the ship was for me.

A blackbird singing
I hear in my troubled mind,
Bluebells swinging
I see in a distant wind.
But sorrow and silence
Are the wood's threnody,
The silence for you
And the sorrow for me.

(In Hospital In Egypt)

SKREEN CROSS ROADS

Five roads meet on the hill of Skreen,
Five fair ways to wander down.
One road sings of the valleys green
Two of the Sea, and one of the town.
And one little road has never a song
Tho' the world be fair and the day be long.

This is the song the south road sings:
"I go where Love and Peace abide.
I pass the world's seven wondrous things
And cities fallen in their pride.
Sunny are the miles thro' which I stray
From the Southern Cross to the Milky Way."

But for all its song is so sweet to hear
It has no melody for my ear.

This is the song the sea roads sings:
"When the moon is full the tide is high;
And the little ships in the harbours swing
When the sea-birds tell that a storm is nigh,
And "Heave" the sailor calls, and "Ho!"
It is far to my love when the strong winds blow."

Oh the lure of the roads that sing of the sea
Make my heart beat fast 'till it broke in me.

This is the song of the road to the town:
"Row by row stand the silent lights,
And the music of bells goes up and down
The slopes of the wind, and high delights

Lure in the folk from the valley farms.
It pulls down the hills with its great grey arms."

It sings its song so low and sweet
That once or twice it has lured my feet.

But the dumb little road that winds to the north
Is the dearest road in the world to me.
I would give my soul – for what it is worth –
To be there in its silent company,
Telling it over my hopes and fears,
With only its silence consoling my ears.

C.P.
(*In Hospital in Egypt, 3 April 1916*)

THOMAS McDONAGH

He shall not hear the bittern cry
In the wild sky, where he is lain,
Nor voices of the sweeter birds
Above the wailing of the rain.

Nor shall he know when loud March blows
Thro' slanting snows her fanfare shrill,
Blowing to flame the golden cup
Of many an upset daffodil.

But when the Dark Cow leaves the moor,
And pastures poor with greedy weeds,
Perhaps he'll hear her low at morn
Lifting her horn in pleasant meads.

(*In Barracks*)

THE BLACKBIRDS

I heard the Poor Old Woman say:
"At break of day the fowler came,
And took my blackbirds from their songs
Who loved me well thro' shame and blame.

No more from lovely distances
Their songs shall bless me mile by mile,
Nor to white Ashbourne call me down
To wear my crown another while.

When bended flowers the angels mark
For the skylark the place they lie,
From there its little family
Shall dip their wings first in the sky.

And when the first surprise of flight
Sweet songs excite, from the far dawn
Shall there come blackbirds loud with love,
Sweet echoes of the singers gone.

But in the lonely hush of eve
Weeping I grieve the silent bills."
I heard the Poor Old Woman say
In Derry of the little hills.

(In Barracks)

FATE

Lugh made a stir in the air
With his sword of cries,
And fairies thro' hidden ways
Came from the skies,
And their spells withered up the fair
And vanquished the wise.

And old lame Balor came down
With his gorgon eye
Hidden behind its lid,
Old, withered and dry.
He looked on the wattle town,
And the town passed by.

These things I know in my dreams,
The crying sword of Lugh,
And Balor's ancient eye
Searching me through,
Withering up my songs
And my pipe yet new.

(In Barracks)

AT CURRABWEE

Every night at Currabwee
Little men with leather hats
Mend the boots of Faery
From the tough wings of the bats.
So my mother told to me,
And she is wise you will agree.

Louder than a cricket's wing
All night long their hammer's glee
Times the merry songs they sing
Of Ireland glorious and free.
So I heard Joseph Plunkett say,
You know he heard them but last May.

And when the night is very cold
They warm their hands against the light
Of stars that make the waters gold
Where they are labouring all the night.
So Pearse said, and he knew the truth,
Among the stars he spent his youth.

And I, myself, have often heard
Their singing as the stars went by,
For am I not of those who reared
The banner of old Ireland high,
From Dublin town to Turkey's shores,
And where the Vardar loudly roars?

C.P.

LAST SONGS
(1918)

AT EVENING

A broad field at a wood's high end,
Daylight out and the stars half lit,
And let the dark-winged bat go flit
About the river's wide blue bend.
But thoughts of someone once a friend
Shall be calling loud thro' the hills of Time.

Wide is the back-door of the Past
And I shall be leaving the slated town.
But no, the rain will be slanting brown
And large drops chasing the small ones fast
Down the wide pane, for a cloud was cast
On youth when he started the world to climb.

There won't be song, for song has died.
There won't be flowers for the flowers are done.
I shall see the red of a large cold sun
Wash down on the slow blue tide,
Where the noiseless deep fish glide
In the dark wet shade of the heavy lime.

C.P.

TO A SPARROW

Because you have no fear to mingle
Wings with those of greater part,
So like me, with song I single
Your sweet impudence of heart.

And when prouder feathers go where
Summer holds her leafy show,
You still come to us from nowhere
Like grey leaves across the snow.

In back ways where odd and end go
To your meals you drop down sure,
Knowing every broken window
Of the hospitable poor.

There is no bird half so harmless,
None so sweetly rude as you,
None so common and so charmless,
None of virtues nude as you.

But for all your faults I love you,
For you linger with us still,
Though the wintry winds reprove you
And the snow is on the hill.

HAD I A GOLDEN POUND
(After the Irish)

Had I a golden pound to spend,
My love should mend and sew no more.
And I would buy her a little quern,
Easy to turn on the kitchen floor.

And for her windows curtains white,
With birds in flight and flowers in bloom,
To face with pride the road to town,
And mellow down her sunlit room.

And with the silver change we'd prove
The truth of Love to life's own end,
With hearts the years could but embolden,
Had I a golden pound to spend.

AFTER COURT MARTIAL

My mind is not my mind, therefore
I take no heed of what men say,
I lived ten thousands years before
God cursed the town of Nineveh.

The Present is a dream I see
Of horror and loud sufferings,
At dawn a bird will waken me
Unto my place among the kings.

And though men called me a vile name,
And all my dream companions gone,
'Tis I the soldier bears the shame,
Not I the king of Babylon.

THE COBBLER OF SARI GUEUL

A cobbler lives in Sari Gueul
Who has a wise mind, people say.
He sits in his door on a three-legged stool,
Hammering leather all the day.
He laughs with the boys who make such noise
And loves to watch how the children play.
Gladly I'd shuffle my lot in a pool
With that of the cobbler of Sari Gueul.

Sorrow to him is a ball of wax
That melts in the sun of a cheerful smile
And all his needs are, a box of tacks,
Thread and leather, old boots in a pile.
I would give my art for half of his heart.
Who wants the world with all its guile?
And which of us two is the greater fool,
Me, or the cobbler of Sari Gueul?

At evening an old cow climbs the street,
So lean and bony you'd wonder how.
He hears the old cracked bell from his seat
And the wrinkles move on his yellow brow,
And he says as he strikes, "To me or my likes
You are coming faster, old brown cow.
Slow steps come fast to the knife and rule."
Says the wise old cobbler of Sari Gueul.

Often I hear him in my sleep,
Hammering still in the little town.
And I see the queer old shops on the steep,
And the queerer folk move up and down.

And the cobbler's sign creaks up in a vine,
When the wind slips over the housetops brown.
Waking, I pray to the Gods who rule
For the queer old cobbler of Sari Gueul.

C.P.

HOME

A burst of sudden wings at dawn,
Faint voices in a dreamy noon,
Evenings of mist and murmurings,
And nights with rainbows of the moon.

And through these things a wood-way dim,
And waters dim, and slow sheep seen
On uphill paths that wind away
Through summer sounds and harvest green.

This is a song a robin sang
This morning on a broken tree,
It was about the little fields
That call across the world to me.

THE DEAD KINGS

All the dead kings came to me
At Rosnaree, where I was dreaming,
A few stars glimmered through the morn,
And down the thorn the dews were streaming.

And every dead king had a story
Of ancient glory, sweetly told.
It was too early for the lark,
But the starry dark had tints of gold.

I listened to the sorrows three
Of that Eire passed into song.
A cock crowed near a hazel croft,
And up aloft dim larks winged strong.

And I, too, told the kings a story
Of later glory, her fourth sorrow:
There was a sound like moving shields
In high green fields and the lowland furrow.

And one said: "We who yet are kings
Have heard these things lamenting inly."
Sweet music flowed from many a bill
And on the hill the morn stood queenly.

And one said: "Over is the singing,
And bell bough ringing, whence we come;
With heavy hearts we'll tread the shadows,
In honey meadows birds are dumb."

And one said: "Since the poets perished
And all they cherished in the way,
Their thoughts unsung, like petal showers
Inflame the hours of blue and grey."

And one said: "A loud tramp of men
We'll hear again at Rosnaree."
A bomb burst near me where I lay.
I woke, 'twas day in Picardy.

TO ONE WHO COMES NOW AND THEN

When you come in, it seems a brighter fire
Crackles upon the hearth invitingly,
The household routine which was wont to tire
Grows full of novelty.

You sit upon our home-upholstered chair
And talk of matters wonderful and strange,
Of books, and travel, customs old which dare
The gods of Time and Change:

Till we with inner word our care refute
Laughing that this our bosoms yet assails,
While there are maidens dancing to a flute
In Andalusian vales.

And sometimes from my shelf of poems you take
And secret meanings to our hearts disclose,
As when the winds of June the mid bush shake
We see the hidden rose.

And when the shadows muster, and each tree
A moment flutters, full of shutting wings,
You take the fiddle and mysteriously
Wake wonders on the strings.

And in my garden, grey with misty flowers,
Low echoes fainter than a beetle's horn
Fill all the corners with it, like sweet showers
Of bells, in the owl's morn.

Come often, friend; with welcome and surprise
We'll greet you from the sea or from the town;
Come when you like and from whatever skies
Above you smile or frown.

(Belgium, 22 July, 1917)

SOLILOQUY

When I was young I had a care
Lest I should cheat me of my share
Of that which makes it sweet to strive
For life, and dying still survive,
A name in sunshine written higher
Than lark or poet dare aspire.

But I grew weary doing well;
Besides, 'twas sweeter in that hell,
Down with the loud banditti people
Who robbed the orchards, climbed the steeple
For jackdaw's eggs and made the cock
Crow ere 'twas daylight on the clock.
I was so very bad the neighbours
Spoke of me at their daily labours.
And now I'm drinking wine in France
The helpless child of circumstance.
To-morrow will be loud with war,
How will I be accounted for?

It is too late now to retrieve
A fallen dream, too late to grieve
A name unmade, but not too late
To thank the gods for what is great;
A keen-edged sword, a soldier's heart,
Is greater than a poet's art.
And greater than a poet's fame
A little grave that has no name,
Whence honour turns away in shame.

WITH FLOWERS

These have more language than my song,
Take them and let them speak for me.
I whispered them a secret thing
Down the green lanes of Allary.

You shall remember quiet ways
Watching them fade, and quiet eyes,
And two hearts given up to love,
A foolish and an overwise.

A SOLDIER'S GRAVE

Then in the lull of midnight, gentle arms
Lifted him slowly down the slopes of death,
Lest he should hear again the mad alarms
Of battle, dying moans, and painful breath.

And where the earth was soft for flowers we made
A grave for him that he might better rest.
So, Spring shall come and leave it sweet arrayed,
And there the lark shall turn her dewy nest.

C.P.

POSTSCRIPT

IN MEMORIAM FRANCIS LEDWIDGE
Killed in France 31 July 1917

The bronze soldier hitches a bronze cape
That crumples stiffly in imagined wind
No matter how the real winds buff and sweep
His sudden hunkering run, forever craned

Over Flanders. Helmet and haversack,
The gun's firm slope from butt to bayonet,
The loyal, fallen names on the embossed plaque –
It all meant little to the worried pet

I was in nineteen forty-six or seven,
Gripping my Aunt Mary by the hand
Along the Portstewart prom, then round the crescent
To thread the Castle Walk out to the strand.

The pilot from Coleraine sailed to the coal-boat.
Courting couples rose out of the scooped dunes.
A farmer stripped to his studs and shiny waistcoat
Rolled the trousers down on his timid shins.

Francis Ledwidge, you courted at the seaside
Beyond Drogheda one Sunday afternoon.
Literary, sweet-talking, countrified,
You pedalled out the leafy road from Slane

Where you belonged, among the dolorous
And lovely: the May altar of wild flowers,
Easter water sprinkled in outhouses,
Mass-rocks and hill-top raths and raftered byres.

I think of you in your Tommy's uniform,
A haunted Catholic face, pallid and brave,
Ghosting the trenches like a bloom of hawthorn
Or silence cored from a Boyne passage-grave.

It's summer, nineteen-fifteen. I see the girl
My aunt was then, herding on the long acre.
Behind a low bush in the Dardanelles
You suck stones to make your dry mouth water.

It's nineteen-seventeen. She still herds cows
But a big strafe puts the candles out in Ypres:
"My soul is by the Boyne, cutting new meadows ...
My country wears her confirmation dress."

"To be called a British soldier while my country
Has no place among nations ... " You were rent
By shrapnel six weeks later. "I am sorry
That party politics should divide our tents."

In you, our dead enigma, all the strains
Criss-cross in useless equilibrium
And as the wind tunes through this vigilant bronze
I hear again the sure confusing drum

You followed from Boyne water to the Balkans
But miss the twilit note your flute should sound.
You were not keyed or pitched like these true-blue ones
Though all of you consort now underground.

Seamus Heaney